THE POWER OF TIME

7 rules for time management and taking control
of your life

Daniel J. Martin

Note: This book was created with the intention of offering information, suggestions and guidance on different areas of life, including emotional wellbeing, mental health, personal growth and the development of healthy relationships. However, it is in no way a substitute for professional medical attention or counseling from a qualified psychologist or therapist. If you are dealing with serious emotional or mental health issues, we recommend that you seek professional help immediately.

ISBN 978-9916-746-01-1

"Don't count the days, make the days count."

— Muhammad Ali

CONTENTS

DOWNLOAD THE AUDIOBOOK FREE!

*If you would prefer to enjoy **The Power of Time** while you drive, walk or work out...*

Download the audio version totally FREE!

www.danieljmartin.es/audio/pot

Introduction

Have you ever felt like time is slipping away from you? Do you have a thousand things to do and no idea where to start? Do you feel you can't finish all the things you start? If so, you're not alone. Time management is a skill that many people find difficult to master, but it's crucial to achieving your goals and living a full and rewarding life.

Our lives are made up of time. In fact, everything in the world is made of time: the careers of people you admire, the food you cooked today, Gothic cathedrals...it all takes time. And time spent doing something never comes back: you can't recycle it, so it's important to use it meaningfully instead of wasting it or simply letting it go by.

Managing the time we have is like playing a card game: once you play a card, you can't take it back, so you need to weigh up your options before every play.

Once you turn 18 (or, I would say, even before then), it's your responsibility to try to make the most of your time: your future and your happiness depend on it. And, although it's hard to see right now, I can promise you that you have more freedom than you think when it comes to managing your time.

Lots of my patients protest when I say that. They're partly right: I know we can't do exactly what we want with our time whenever we want. Every morning when we wake up, we have to eat breakfast and rush around getting ready for work, going to meetings, reviewing budgets, enduring traffic and doing lots of other things we would rather not do. I'm aware that you can't just lie there and sip piña colada while other people do all your work for you. But I also know that we all waste a lot more time than is strictly necessary by not making good choices.

Time is not easy to manage, but fortunately, just like any other task, you can learn to do it. If you learn to manage your time, you'll be the master of your life. And to learn to manage time, first you need to ask yourself the right questions: what do you want to manage it for? In what direction? What do you want to achieve?

We will go into depth on these and other questions over the course of this book. Because you won't achieve happiness if you don't decide in advance what your intentions, goals and current situation are. If you're not aware, you will end up living an aimless life, going with the flow without knowing why you do what you do or where the days are going.

Wise people know the value of time. Good leaders and happy people do, too. They all plan their goals in advance and make the most of every minute of their lives. Because the truth is that the time will pass whether you take advantage of it or not.

On top of all this, time management is also closely linked to your physical and mental health. So, if you don't keep your workflow under control, the dozens of tasks you have to complete each day will become a source of great stress and exhaustion. You will always be rushing to catch up, improvising strategies to get back lost time and missing out on opportunities. In other words, while good time management brings you benefits, failing to manage your time will leave you in a clearly negative situation.

Not managing your time has terrible consequences that, sooner or later, will take their toll. I'm not telling you this to discourage you or scare you: I'm telling you because changing the situation is within your reach.

I also know what it means not to fulfil your commitments. I know that feeling of powerlessness that comes from yet another monumental waste of time due to poor planning. I know the feeling of guilt that grows when the days pass by without achieving anything and without knowing where to begin. I know because, like you, I've been there.

When I was a teenager, my time management was conspicuous in its absence. The days simply passed by while I got distracted by every little thing and kept putting off important tasks, the ones with the power to improve my future, over and over again.

Fortunately, the empty feeling that gave me pushed me to find the common tools and strategies that more successful and personally satisfied people have shared throughout history.

It wasn't an easy journey, but it was worth it. Nowadays, I can say that I manage, as Golda Meir[1] put it, to "govern the clock, not be governed by it."

How did I do it?

Basically, I discovered that effective time management rests on four pillars:

1. **Knowing what stage I'm at**, including my current obligations and the objectives I want to achieve.

2. **Planning my days around routines** that balance out the two previous points (obligations and objectives).

3. **Categorize and order each new task** depending on its importance and/or urgency.

---

1 Golda Meir was Israel's first female prime minister: a post she held for ten years.

4. **Focusing all my attention on one task** at a time.

By following these steps, I designed 7 **definitive rules for time management**. Seven rules based on years of experience and studies into time management, productivity and the psychology of success, which I have successfully applied to hundreds of patients before finally deciding to write this book so that thousands or millions of people can benefit from its surprising results.

Whether you need to improve your work output or make time for a new activity, whether you've encountered a real "time thief" or you simply want to lead a calmer, more relaxed life, these 7 rules are for you.

What can you expect from this book?

I want you to take this book as an investment in your future. Maybe one of the best investments you'll make in your life.

All you need to get started is the right attitude. Set aside any prejudices you have toward self-help books that promise miracles: what I'm offering here is a collection of concepts and tools that are totally practical, easy to understand and even easier to apply. I'm not selling philosophies, invisible energy or esoteric powers: all you need is the right attitude and a willingness to work. The 7 rules will do the rest. I promise!

Imagine for a moment what your life would be like if you could manage your time effectively. Imagine waking up each morning feeling motivated and energized, knowing that you have a clearly defined plan for the rest of the day. Imagine achieving more in less time, and having more free time to do the things you want to do and spend quality time with the people you love.

If you're still not convinced, read on, because we're just getting started.

Ready? Let's go!

There's no time to lose!

Daniel

Why you should learn to manage your time

"The bad news is time flies. The good news is you're the pilot."

— Michael Altshuler

Imagine you had to move some water from once place to another, quickly, using buckets. On your first trip you fill the buckets up to the brim, so you keep spilling water on your way. You try to go quickly, so by the time you get to where you have to empty the buckets, you're so exhausted that you drop half the water on the ground. On your next trip, you improve your technique: you only fill the buckets halfway and you walk more slowly. You also watch where you're going so you don't trip and you check that the buckets don't have holes in: in other words, you analyze the situation and review your options in order to be as efficient as possible.

It's the same thing with time management: at first, you lose it along the way, and it's only through experience and strategy that you can optimize your energy.

We all have the same twenty-four hours in each day. Even when you know this (there are no surprises here – every day is the same length), you end every day exhausted and not having achieved the tasks you set yourself. That means that either your to-do list was unrealistic, you didn't manage those hours well and "the bull caught up with you", as we say in Spain, or you were exposed to unexpected setbacks.

All those things can happen from time to time, but not all the time: if you are busy all day but always left with unfinished tasks, if you're not making time to rest or enjoy things, then you need to hit the brakes and review the situation.

The importance of highlighting time management

Why should you organize your life around time and not organize your objectives around your happiness, for example?

It's a good question. The reason is, as we said in the introduction, your goals are made of time. If you don't set your objectives based on measurable time frames, you will fail – it's that simple.

Why? Because time is linear and limited. That's something we often forget: you go to bed, wake up and have a new day ahead of you. That gives you the feeling that you will always have a new day available. Whatever you don't achieve today, you can do tomorrow. And to a certain extent, that's true, but only to a certain extent; the days will end at some point. That's why you always need to bear in mind that the pursuit of your goals requires fragments of time that have a beginning and an end.

In terms of the pursuit of happiness, this is built upon your mental health, which is highly vulnerable to the stress and tiredness caused by poor time management itself.

So learning to manage your time not only enables you to be more productive and efficient – it also helps you grow as a person, contributing to your spiritual development and your happiness.

When you prioritize time management, you're not delaying your happiness, you're actually getting closer to it. Why? Because you're putting into practice a series of skills that pave the way for wellbeing and personal fulfilment.

What effects can good time management have on your life?

In addition to increasing your productivity, it has other advantages, too: all in one package!

1. It increases your self-discipline.

Self-discipline helps you fight against procrastination, distractions and discouragement. In fact, it's one of the basic prerequisites for governing time, since there is no point in planning tasks or habits if you end up abandoning them out of a lack of consistency.

Self-discipline is the fuel that drives your ship and helps you to achieve your scheduled tasks on time.

The more self-disciplined you are, the better you will manage your time, and vice versa.

2. It improves your sleep and your health.

How many of us don't get enough sleep? Or complain about not having enough time for self-care?

So many health complications come from insufficient sleep, lack of exercise or physical neglect. When we have a lot of obligations to fulfil, we sacrifice resting time, ignore doctors' orders, dose up on caffeine, take supplements instead of eating right, and quit working out.

Although all of this leads to a short-time time saving, the time you save by skipping the gym will have to be "paid back" later, with interest. I can promise you that's true. Many of my patients have experienced this for themselves before deciding to make a change (usually, when their bodies send them a wake-up call).

Managing your time means devoting the necessary number of hours to each thing, including sleep and health. Of course, your responsibilities will occasionally keep you up late, or an incident will mean you have to postpone your dentist appointment. Life is long and full of unexpected events. But you can't allow your health to stay permanently on a back burner.

3. It boosts your self-esteem.

Many people are skeptical on this point. They say "But self-esteem is about valuing yourself, not about sticking to a schedule, right?".

It's true. Self-esteem can't rely on memorizing a list of tasks while you eat breakfast in order to fulfil every single one of your commitments. But "self-esteem" also means self-respect. And respect involves valuing your time instead of handing it out to just anybody or spending it on things that end up hindering you. Self-esteem includes not endlessly postponing your doctor's check-up or sacrificing your vacations in order to please others or achieve a warped sense of success.

Self-esteem is respect, and respect means refusing to accept that someone else's time is more important than yours. It doesn't matter if that person is your boss, your neighbor or your bank manager: your time deserves as much respect as anyone else's.

I'm not saying that you shouldn't follow your boss's instructions if that's part of your contract. I'm definitely not saying you should ignore someone who needs you because you suddenly feel like going shopping. That would just be a childish, irresponsible attitude. What I am saying is that you should defend your time and not allow it to be stolen from you.

When you start to respect your time, it will annoy some people. It's a good way of smoking out parasites and users. At first, you might get a few jibes from someone who's used to stealing your time. But it will be worth it. By the end of the year, you will be looking back and thinking: "Have I really achieved all this? Not bad!". This recognition of your achievements will boost your confidence and help develop your self-esteem.

4. It broadens your horizons.

Good time management will also give you the chance to aim higher: you won't have to work twice as hard to earn more, but you can aspire to higher positions.

If you organize yourself well, you will go from spending your life being bossed around to having final say.

If your goal is to grow professionally, you will have time to prepare yourself and take the leap. If you want to achieve a sporting goal, you will know how to focus your training so you get the most out of it, even if you don't have much time. If what you want is to build a solid relationship with your partner but you're always working, time management will help you turn what little time you have with them into quality time.

In short, you will still have twenty-four hours in a day, but you will be able to set yourself more ambitious goals.

5. It improves your personal relationships.

Most psychologists and wellbeing experts endorse the importance of quality affectionate relationships in achieving happiness. I completely agree: your family, partner, friends, children and even pets deserve to share valued moments with you.

When time is short, relationships can be affected and weakened. To avoid this, we often end up giving them low-quality time: we replace moments of full and exclusive attention with hurried phone calls while we do the housework or check our emails. Or maybe we only ask our partners how their day went at bedtime when we're brushing our teeth and setting an alarm, already thinking about what we have to do tomorrow.

Proper time management involves earmarking some time to be **present and aware** with the people you love. You can "be" there in lots of ways, even over the phone, but it's fundamental to focus your attention on the conversation in order for it to be meaningful. I don't mean that when you're chatting to your brother, you have to talk about quantum physics or psychoanalyze each other: what I mean is that the conversation, however brief or informal, needs to be authentic and in keeping with what that person means to you.

When you spend time with someone, regardless of their relationship to you, you should try to give and receive, no matter how little. Depending on the level of closeness to them, remember to ask how their job interview went, thank them for something they did for you, or share an anecdote you know will make them laugh. If there is more intimacy between you, you should honor that bond and go into depth in your commitment to them.

6. **It helps you make good decisions.**

Making the right decision doesn't depend solely on the information you have. It also takes time to reflect and visualize possible scenarios and consequences before taking the next step.

Time management involves devoting the necessary hours to making each decision in a calm, confident way. Mistakes are always possible, sure, but the risk is much less this way, as is the chance of regretting something down the line. The opposite of this is making decisions under pressure or led by impulsiveness or improvisation: three weapons of the devil.

It's true that decision-making isn't everyone's strong point, but it's a skill that can be learned and trained: if you need a week to make a decision the first time, you'll need less than a week the second time, even if the context is different.

It's worth learning how to make decisions, and you can only do it if you're brave enough not just to take that step but also to take the time you need to make the right decisions.

Chapter summary

Why is it so important to learn to manage your time?

—   Because your life is made of time, and time is a resource that may be abundant but is not infinite. The sooner you understand that, the sooner you will start to be more efficient.

—   Not only does good time management help you to be more productive, it also contributes to your personal growth and your self-esteem

—   Time management strengthens your self-discipline.

—   Time management benefits your sleep and physical and mental health.

—   Time management enables you to have more ambitious objectives.

– Time management predisposes you to establish and maintain better affectionate relationships.

– Time management helps you make better decisions.

Create routines

"Take care of the minutes and the hours will take care of themselves."

— Lord Chesterfield

Imagine you're the chef at a restaurant. I'm sure you agree with me that, without good planning for the creation of each dish, you will make more mistakes, it will take more time to fulfil each order and you'll undoubtedly be more stressed at work.

Fortunately, chefs have what is known as a technical datasheet for each dish. These sheets contain detailed information about the dish to be prepared, including the necessary ingredients, required amounts, preparation instructions, cooking time and so on.

Well, these datasheets are routines.

The first rule for effective time management is to divide the day into parts according to your obligations and create a routine for each part: the routine of getting up, the routine of having breakfast, the routine of getting ready to go out, going to work, leaving work...It may seem childlike, but it's amazing how much energy you can save with this method.

Why? Because routines help to automatize processes so that they don't require so much energy or concentration.

Before I learned the importance of routines, I found it hard to get each day started. When I woke up, I found it difficult to get out of bed because I felt like I had to make too many decisions in one go that were fleeting and unrelated to my life goals and aspirations: thinking about what to have for breakfast, what to wear, and so on.

That took me so much time and I was consumed by the knowledge that I should be using that energy on more important things. That's the essence of routines: they are the only way of gaining time through the **automatization of parts of your everyday that are always the same**.

Now, however, I have specific routines for my mornings. That means that when I wake up, I begin the day already knowing what I need to do. I don't have to stay in bed deciding where to start.

My whole day follows this pattern. I have a basic pattern of routines that I can complete or modify with new elements and tasks. In the afternoon, I know exactly what time I stop working (except on occasion) and I start working out, going shopping, seeing friends or doing leisure activities.

Of course, unexpected events come up. And a normal Monday routine is not going to be the same as the first day of your vacation. But if most of your day is organized into routines, you will find it much easier to tackle both the known and the unknown.

Benefits of organizing your everyday into routines:

- **Routines help you keep control over your time**, and to get it back faster if you lose it at some point.

- **Routines will enable you to calibrate the time you devote to each task** more easily, avoiding delays and accumulations. When you order your life around routines, you'll know how much time each thing takes you, and what moments of your day enable you to include more or less workflow.

- **Routines will bring you order**. The less noise and chaos there is around you (whether it's physical or mental), the more efficient you'll be and the more wellbeing you'll find in your life.

- **Routines will help you tackle emergencies**. Whether it's an illness, an unexpected appointment or a task that requires immediate attention, having routines will help you to take on surprises. Without them, you'll make bad decisions and a single incident can derail the rest of your day.

- **Routines lower your risk of losing or forgetting things:** objects, tasks, dates or long-term objectives, routines will help you stay focused because you won't have to mentally check so many things. If you always have to remember things, your risk of making mistakes goes through the roof.

- **Routines help you to ignore distractions and temptations.** When we're tired or overwhelmed, the impulse to procrastinate is too strong to hold off. When you have a fixed routine, it's easy to go onto autopilot if you're tired instead of procrastinating because you don't have enough energy or motivation.

- **Routines are like working out: you get better and better at them.** Given that they are actions you repeat, you will be able to carry them out a little better each time, in less time and using less mental effort.

Tips for creating routines

How do you divide your day into routines and construct them all? Let's break it down into steps:

1. **Study yourself and take note of what you do each day** and how long each activity takes you: showering, eating breakfast, getting to work, eating, and so on.

2. **Decide if you're spending the right amount of time on each thing,** or if it should be taking you more or less time. Figure

out why you don't do it that way and how to correct it (this may take some trial and error).

3. **Divide your day into time slots** in accordance with the above points. My advice is to do this in 4 parts:

   - The morning before you start working.

   - Work until lunchtime.

   - Work after lunchtime.

   - From when you finish your working day to when you go to bed.

4. **Establish short routines** for each of these slots – the more detailed, the better. Make things easy on yourself so you can automatize as many actions as you can, from the ingredients for your breakfast to your gym bag or getting your paperwork ready.

5. **Create a time limit** for each of your routines. At first you will find it annoying to have so many "rules", but then it will come

naturally to you and you will have saved a ton of time.

6. **Create a plan for emergencies or unforeseen events**. Where do you put the tasks you didn't complete today? Set aside a couple of hours a week for unexpected events, one-off actions, reminders, and so on.

7. **Be generous with your rest time and realistic with deadlines**. Making the most of your time doesn't mean sleeping four hours a night, having breakfast on the subway or skim-reading reports. It's very important to be realistic about the amount of time you need for each thing.

8. **Find ways to strengthen your motivation** for tasks you find harder: from small rewards for each unpleasant task you complete to free time, even in the middle of your working day.

9. **Get used to getting up early**. Morning is the most important routine of the day. It's the

one that will dictate how the rest of your day goes. If you make your morning routine a good one, you will be in the best position for completing the rest of your routines until you go to bed. On the other hand, if you start the day by skipping or prolonging your early routines, you will be behind for the rest of the day.

Chapter summary

Why should you divide your day into short, joined-up routines?

– Routines are an essential tool for saving time and energy, because they enable you to automatize processes that you repeat in order not to have to give them so much of your attention.

– When you put tasks that don't require all your energy on autopilot, routines reduce the risk of distractions, procrastination or lack of motivation.

– Routines help you regain control more quickly after a setback.

– Routines help you stay focused on more important tasks: those that require all your attention and that add value to your objectives.

– To create routines that work, first you need to study your everyday life to figure out what your needs are and which tasks are repeated. Then, you should set a specific amount of time aside for carrying out each task, and adapt to your plan. In time, you'll find following your routines comes naturally.

Act now

"You may delay, but time will not."
— Benjamin Franklin

Let's play a game.

Imagine that every morning, when you wake up, I have put $1,440 into your bank account to spend however you choose. You don't have to give me any explanations or do anything you don't want. The only condition is that, by the end of the day, anything you didn't spend that day will be removed from your account.

What do you think of this gift? Do you feel like making the most of all that free money?

Well, you don't actually have $1,440 every day in your account, but you do have 1,440 minutes to use when you open your eyes each morning.

Are you going to make the most of them, or let them pass you by?

The inner voice that tells you to put things off

Yes, we want to make the most of our time, but it's hard when even your own brain is working against you.

Humans tend toward inactivity. Instinctively, if we have the choice between inaction and movement, we opt for the former. It's not that we're lazy, idle or afraid (or maybe it is): it's our lizard brain. It still works like our distant ancestors' did, and it's driven by survival instinct.

Our brains tell us something like: "Do you really have to do that? You're doing fine so far – why change anything?"

That's right! The human mind is designed to seek instant gratification for minimal effort as a way of preserving our lives. In its keenness to stay in its comfort zone, our brains invite us to skip out on obligations or spend "bad" time on them (you know, half-ass things and not give them our full attention).

This means that, if we're not careful, the human brain will always opt for the easiest and most agreeable option. That's why it prefers playing over working. That's why it prefers tasks with a close and tangible end instead of long-term ones. All of it brings instant gratification and security.

However, we know that hurts us in the long run. So why do we procrastinate?

There have been many studies into the causes of procrastination. In general terms, we can conclude that we procrastinate when the task doesn't guarantee short-term satisfaction or security. This might be because it's complex, because we don't understand it or because it requires a lot of energy. The mind registers that activity as unappealing and it looks for alternatives and excuses dressed up as more useful or urgent tasks (sometimes it doesn't even do that).

In other cases, it's the result of a task "well done" that we're afraid of, so we procrastinate out of a fear of success. We'll look at that later.

Consequences of living in procrastination mode

You don't need a lot of insight to be able to see that procrastination is something that you can't afford: there's too much at stake. However, it gives you the idea that wasting an entire Sunday afternoon lying on the couch is not that big a deal. And it's not, as long as that what you decided to do beforehand.

Relaxing is not the same as procrastinating: procrastinating is doing one thing knowing that you should be doing another. It's shirking your responsibilities. And sooner or later, that will come back to bite you.

– **When you procrastinate, you're creating problems that didn't exist before** and that will be harder to resolve later. When you postpone an unappealing task, you feel a fleeting sense of satisfaction, but that task is still there. It doesn't disappear, it doesn't let you off the hook, and you can't get rid of it without doing it.

"There's still time," you tell yourself. Until your time is up, and you start to panic: you have to ask for an extension, you have to invent excuses, you have to do the task quickly and poorly, and you have to apologize for it. You have to put off other things in order to tackle that eleventh-hour task.

Procrastination creates a dangerous snowball that keeps growing and picking up speed as it hurtles down the mountainside.

–   **When you procrastinate, you block the next level**. The fact that task is still on your horizon stops you from thinking further ahead, so you lose your ability to focus on the goals that come next and those you have for the long term.

–   **When you procrastinate, you become an untrustworthy person**. If you set out to do something, if you're committed to a task, ignoring it or not doing it proves that you don't always show up when you need to. And that will hurt you both in your work and your personal life.

–   **When you procrastinate, you become mediocre**. When you put something off, you give laziness a greater chance of beating you, both at that task and at others. That turns you into a mediocre person. Into someone who settles for the minimum, who refuses to seek excellence or to feel passionate about their job or their life. The best careers and the happiest lives are never mediocre.

– **When you procrastinate, you're trying to hide your own fears from yourself**. Those fears, like the snowball we talked about, will only get bigger the longer it takes you to face them. If you tend to turn in your reports late, you become an inefficient worker. Have you ever asked yourself why you do it? Maybe, deep down, what you want is to make sure no one thinks of you when a job opportunity comes up: you're afraid of being better.

Have you heard of imposter syndrome?

Basically, it consists of sabotaging yourself out of fear of accepting responsibility for your entire potential.

When you procrastinate, not only are you living beneath your potential: you're giving in to indifference, conformism and, over time, to negativity and resentment.

How to procrastinate less

Alright! I won't procrastinate again! But how do you do that?

There isn't, but it's been proven that procrastination disappears when there is:

- A lot of willpower backing up your intention to complete a task.

- A clear and powerful reason for doing something, or very bad consequences if you don't.

- A clear and simple method or routine for tackling the task, or good planning.

- A more than 70% chance of success.

- A clear reward, in the form of a prize or personal satisfaction, based on the importance of fulfilling that task.

- A good physical and mental condition.

- An environment that fosters that behavior, rather than the opposite (behavior is "contagious").

All this explains, for example, why a difficult sporting goal is more attractive than ironing clothes: neither the motivation nor the satisfaction of one of those tasks can be compared to the other.

How to tackle procrastination

Before you learn some strategies for beating procrastination, you should take a look at the way you act and detect your bad habits to figure out why you have them and how you can eliminate them. For example, the habit of lazing around in bed for ages before getting up.

1. **Figure out what you're trying to avoid.**

What makes you not want to get up when your alarm goes off? What's out there that's so threatening or so unappealing? What turns your good intentions into excuses?

Most of us procrastinate because we subconsciously fear the task ahead of us.

2. Change the way you look at that task.

Once you understand why you're afraid or reluctant to complete that task (sometimes, rather than one single reason, it's several), you should perform an empathy exercise with yourself (yes, empathize with the lazing around in bed) and accept that that procrastination is an attempt to protect yourself from something. It's a (bad) defense mechanism.

Then, you need to counteract that logic that you want to get rid of using weighty arguments you really believe in. Your brain should be able to see the undeniable advantages of changing.

For example, if you've decided to quit being a couch potato, think about what you can offer your brain so that it wants to get up as soon as it hears your alarm. Bear in mind, your offering needs to be powerful. If you have decided to get up earlier because you want to have "more time for breakfast", I doubt your new habit will stick. Why? Because it's not strong enough. Your brain will tell you: "If we've survived this long having a quick breakfast, why change now? Let's stay in bed a little longer."

No – your new argument needs to be much stronger than that. If necessary, it can come with consequences. For example, if you've decided that for every minute you lounge around in bed you're going to give ten dollars to a stranger, you'll find that changes things pretty quickly.

3. Divide that task into mini-tasks that are much smaller and more accessible.

If you've decided to write your first novel, don't view it as a single, mammoth task, but as a puzzle to be completed piece by piece. Focus on each piece, on each little accomplishment, and you'll find it easier to keep going every day.

4. Pass the point of no return.

What I call the point of no return tends to be the first step of a task, although sometimes it comes later. In any case, it's the point past which you can no longer give up. Once you've taken that step, you will find it hurts more to quit than to keep going. For example, continuing with the example of the novel, the point of no return is signing a contract with an editor, or announcing the launch on your socials, or maybe signing up the title of your novel at a convention or challenge.

5. Change the habits that foster procrastination.

Just like my suggestion of turning wasted minutes into dollars, you should find strategies for every harmful habit you want to eliminate.

Sometimes it works to introduce a substitute habit: another activity that occupies the time the bad habit occupied before. Sometimes, it takes "extreme measures", like leaving your phone outside your room so you have to get out of bed or you have to go to bed earlier and stay there whether you're asleep or not, and so on.

6. Visualize your objectives often.

Something else I recommend is to keep your dreams and aspirations in mind. If you've decided to change jobs, but you need training, that can become a good reason to get up out of bed earlier and use the time to read. Remind yourself of that every time your alarm goes off and you want to hit snooze.

7. Don't be afraid of difficult tasks.

One excuse for procrastination is that the task is too demanding and requires energy you just don't have right now. However, those kinds of tasks tend to be the most worthwhile and beneficial in the long run.

To combat fear of a task, you need to face it with courage and common sense. Will putting it off make it easier to do? Or will someone come along and do it for you? Instead of going through the stress of procrastinating while constantly thinking about what you have to do, tackle the task and feel the thrill of crossing it off your to-do list.

8. Prioritize your planned schedule ahead of unexpected events.

Surprise circumstances are bound to crop up, and when they do, they will probably affect your planned schedule. While you're trying to decide whether to do the task you had planned or tackle the unforeseen situation, procrastination can rear its head and delay both tasks. Decide on one and don't look back: if the situation means you have to take care of the setback first, do it. If not, prioritize your schedule. But don't stop moving!

9. Commit to an anti-procrastination buddy.

A responsibility buddy can be a big help. If you have decided to write five hundred words of your novel each day, find someone you don't want to disappoint and call them every day that you don't hit your word count to confess.

Chapter summary

–   Each new day, you have 1,440 minutes to spend as you please.

–   If you don't use them wisely, procrastination, the thief of time, will eat away at your life.

–   Procrastination is a toxic dynamic that tends to keep going if we don't stop it. It's a bad habit and, like them all, it's addictive and hard to eliminate because it gives a false and temporary sense of freedom.

–   Procrastination tends to be underpinned by a fear of failure, or sometimes a fear of success. In either case, it's not worth it.

–   To stop it in its tracks, you need to follow your routines strictly and eliminate as much as possible any distractions, bearing in mind the consequences of inaction and remembering the kind of person you become when you procrastinate.

–   There are many strategies for hitting the brakes on procrastination, from the point of no return to commitment to other people. Anything goes if it helps you stop looking for excuses to postpone or quit something.

Forward planning

"He, who every morning plans the transactions of that day, and follows that plan, carries a thread that will guide him through a labyrinth of the most busy life."

— Victor Hugo

Planning is the only way to keep your day under control. Planning means preparing the day, week or year with intention and based on clear objectives: your objectives!

Why is planning so important? Well, there is one main reason: if you don't plan your day according to your interests, you will end up devoting your day to the interests of others. And it's not just me who says that: Jim Rohn, famous American businessman and motivational speaker, said it too. "If you don't design your own life plan, chances are you'll fall into someone else's plan. And guess what they have planned for you? Not much."

We know that not everything we plan will turn out exactly how we pictured it. Not all our objectives are going to come true just because we decided on them in advance (we're not gods and we can't see the future), but we can reduce the margins of uncertainty and improvise.

If planning has so many benefits, why don't people do it? Or do it...by halves?

I believe that the main obstacle is that it requires quality time and resources (information, results forecasts, experience, and so on) in order to plan properly. Sometimes, that time is viewed as unnecessary or even as a weakness ("do you really need to plan everything in so much detail? Can't you just remember stuff?") But all the effort you put into it is worth it. In the words of the pioneer Dale Carnegie[2]: "An hour of planning can save you ten hours of doing."

How good planning saves you time and energy

At some point, we have all gone onto autopilot or chaos mode: making minimal decisions, going with the flow without looking beyond, waiting for "a better moment". That's valid – or even inevitable – in times of temporary crisis, but not permanently: the long-term outcome of this is a mechanical lifestyle without intent and where the balance between effort and benefit is totally out of whack.

As a therapist and life coach, part of my job consists of opening people's eyes to the fact that they're living beneath their potential. They're wasting time and opportunities because they

---

[2] Dale Carnegie was an American writer and businessman and the author of several books and theories on human relations. He endorsed what is now known as *responsibility assumption.*

have not stopped to look at their control panel before starting to operate their machinery.

Many of my patients complain when I ask them to plan. They say that their everyday lives are already set to guidelines consisting of work, housework, kids, working out when they can, and not a lot more. There isn't much to plan because everything is fixed in advance. And they're partly right. But it's also true that, if you take a magnifying glass to your hours as if they were pipework in a building, you would find more than one crack where water is leaking out. And, following this metaphor, you would also find some blocked pipes and others that don't lead anywhere. You might even find that some wise guy has tampered with one of your pipes so he can take your water.

The benefits of good planning

- **Planning as a tool for creating for priorities.**

Planning also means deciding what's urgent, what's important, what's an absolute priority and what's an emergency. If you analyze your everyday life, you'll realize that your tasks don't make sense in terms of importance; many are low priority, but for some reason (they're easier to do, they're comfortable, everyone does them that way, and so on) they jump ahead of the important ones.

In the next chapter (Rule number 4), we'll talk about this.

– Planning as an "irregularity detector".

When your everyday life is so full that you couldn't slide a pin in it, you need to start reviewing and sacrificing activities. And no, those activities should not be hours of sleep or leisure (unless you have too many of them), but activities that don't bring you anything. Activities you do out of habit, because they are expected of you or because you're "the only one who knows how to do it". There are tasks you have taken on but which, by rights, should be done by someone else.

It might be uncomfortable or violent, but you have to start delegating and insisting on a fairer distribution of tasks if you're doing more than your fair share (and others are reaping the benefits). All of this tends to go unnoticed if you don't plan.

- **Planning as a way to eliminate distractions.**

We have already talked about procrastination, and a lack of planning facilitates those "leaks". On the other hand, when your schedule is carefully designed, it's harder for you to get lost because all you have to do is take a look at your agenda in order to know if you're doing what you're supposed to be doing. Planning makes it less likely that you'll waste your time or, even worse, spend it on activities that sabotage your interests.

A few years ago, I used to go for dinner with a friend of mine, Paul, every Friday. Paul and I are aficionados of movies and series, so every Friday we would drag dinner out in order to discuss the series we were watching or the last movie we saw at the theater. We knew it was getting late, but it was Friday after all!

It was only when I started making schedules that I realized that those dinners would easily take up more than two hours!

When I told Paul this, he was surprised, too. We decided to chat for less time and make it one Saturday a month instead.

Something similar happens with social media: I think they can be amazing tools for staying connected to friends and family, for learning about topics that interest us, for laughing, relaxing, staying up-to-date and so on. However, it's only when you look at the numbers of minutes a day you spend on these apps that you realize the real size of the iceberg.

I'm sure that you have distractions that crop up often that you just haven't noticed yet. As part of your planning, I advise you to locate these and take them into account.

– **Planning against unrealistic visions of your aspirations.**

Planning is an act of self-discovery. While you're designing your plan and reflecting on what you need to do to achieve it, you discover which aspirations are realistic and which are fantasy. Which timeframes are impossible and which are reasonable. You may even discover that one of your goals is not what you really want.

Sun Tzu [3] claimed that you can figure out whether you will win or lose a battle before beginning by analyzing your strengths and those of your enemy and drawing conclusions. In the same way, your planning shows you your chances of success before beginning the battle, saving you an enormous amount of time and energy.

– Planning as a thermometer for your achievements.

The only way to know if you're getting closer to your goals is to plan what they are and when they should be completed. Only when you have a plan do you begin to know if you're reaching your goals or moving away from them. Without that, it's easy to get lost along the way and forget your destination.

---

[3] General and philosopher of Ancient Imperial China, prior to J.C. and famous for his essay *The Art of War*.

When your day is planned in advance, every night you will be able to see if you are fulfilling the tasks you planned or if you need to adjust your routines. If you don't plan, you'll make the same mistakes again in the long term.

- **Planning against discouragement, self-sabotage and fear.**

Planning your time not only helps you with unrealistic expectations, it also gives you confidence in the face of dips in mood. When you're tired or not seeing good results, you may get tempted to quit; the more solid your plan, the harder it will be to throw in the towel.

In addition, planning makes tasks seem easier and more accessible because it forces some visualization work first. Planning gives you a sense of control that's already an advantage in itself.

- **Planning versus "freedom".**

Some people criticize plans because they believe that an excessively planned-out life is unexciting and lacking in spontaneity. Many of my patients say this at the beginning of their process: "I'm going to feel like a robot with all this planning and timing! I want to feel free!".

However, only a good plan enables you to be free, because it's the only thing that can help you optimize your time, money, capacity for work and relationship with your surroundings. Having a good plan will give you more resources for making better decisions and more free time for yourself. That means that planning gives you freedom, while a lack of it give you a false sense of freedom that ends up turning into aimlessness.

How to create a good timetable

A timetable is a plan that tackles a whole day. It contains a specific list of tasks and obligations that you're going to be involved in throughout the day, and the time at which each one should take place.

You can create your timetable on paper, in an agenda or similar, using apps or on your work computer. All you need is for it to be practical and make sense for you.

This is how I recommend you do it:

1. Use a good agenda.

My recommendation for creating a good timetable, that is, the nucleus of your planning (by the hour) is to use a paper agenda[4] given that it's been proven that writing by hand activates different areas of your brain that enable you to process and retain information in a more effective way than typing on a keyboard.

---

[4] I recommend that you don't buy the cheapest or lowest quality agenda, because you'll end up abandoning it, it will break, it will stop being useful, etc.

When you write your timetable in a physical agenda, you are etching the information onto your memory and helping yourself to remember your tasks better.

2. Include all kinds of tasks.

When making your to-do list for the day or week, you should bear in mind the different kinds of tasks (urgent, important, short or long, no end date, and so on) and note these down in your agenda like a chess game or battle plan.

You should also set aside some time each week for attending to unforeseen events and distributing the tasks that only happen once a month or once a year: taking the car to the shop, going to the dentist, paying your taxes, preparing a presentation for your report, and so on. Just because it only happens once doesn't mean it should catch you by surprise.

3. Group small tasks together.

Wherever possible, put together in hour-long blocks the tasks that only take a few minutes: making a phone call, putting a load of laundry in, watering the plants, writing quick emails. This will stop you from wasting a lot of time interrupting longer tasks to attend to these ones.

4. Make and keep some free time.

Free time is necessary, simply put. It's a way to liberate your brain and strengthen relationships and learning, as well as to rest and enjoy life.

Free time shouldn't just be for the weekends, vacations or last few minutes before going to sleep; throughout the day, you should set aside some time where you allow yourself to do nothing. Isn't that wasting time? No, not if those minutes are flanked by some time spent fully concentrating.

So, separate your daily tasks with some brief pauses where you allow yourself to listen to a song, distract yourself for five minutes on social media, read a recipe you'd like to try, or simply sit with your eyes closed.

Free time and rest are so important that, for my method, we're going to dedicate a whole chapter to them (Rule 7).

5. Stick to your schedule.

Of course, you make a timetable in order to stick to it. It's only to be expected that unforeseen circumstances come up, but we've already said that the more detailed your plan, the easier it will be to resume it after a deviation. You shouldn't panic over last-minute changes, but you also shouldn't get your brain used to them, especially when you still have tasks left unfinished because you didn't think about where to relocate them to. You want to make it uncomfortable for you to skip something out of your plan, not the other way around.

Important: your timetable is there to be consulted often throughout your day. It shouldn't be closed from one Sunday to the next. Don't try to exercise your memory all the time; use your schedule to free it up and increase your productivity.

6. Reward yourself at the end of the day.

When you fulfil your schedules for a whole day, treat yourself. A little extra TV time in the evening, a treat, anything that serves as gratification will help your mind to link a positive feeling to your planning.

7. Don't punish yourself if you fail.

Did you spend Sunday planning your days full of hope and find that by Tuesday, things had gone downhill and your plan totally fell apart? Well, these things happen. Be kind to yourself when you fall down. If it was a one-off, resume things when you can and try to fulfil the remainder of your routine. Remember that you can't control the universe, and that perfectionism is more of a problem than a solution.

8. Make it visible: use reminders, alarms and Post-It notes.

Anything goes if it keeps you organized, just like anything goes to free up your memory from things that can be remembered by an agenda or digital calendar. Your brain should focus on working hard in the areas you decide, not on remembering your doctor's appointment, your work meeting, your psychologist assessment or this week's masterclass.

Once you have planned all of that, write it down in your schedule and forget about it until the time comes. You'll feel so free!

Chapter summary

To manage your time well, you need to know how to plan: to schedule tasks in advance in such a way that you can do them all without ending up exhausted.

Planning will also enable you to:

– Create priorities: given that there are only twenty-four hours in a day, you need to fence off the most essential tasks and sacrifice those with less value.

– Detect "irregularities": obsolete tasks that you keep doing, tasks that you do but that should be done by someone else, and so on.

– Eliminate distractions.

– Discover unrealistic visions and objectives.

–   Avoid discouragement when you don't get the results you hoped for: if you trust in your plan, it will be easier to keep going.

–   Know if you're getting closer to or further away from your goals.

Finally, remember that you should preferably plan using a physical, written agenda. Planning "by memory" is not at all recommended: a good agenda (along with digital planners and apps) should be your main weapon.

Prioritize your tasks and objectives

"I have two kinds of problems, the urgent and the important. The urgent are not important, and the important are never urgent."

— Dwight D. Eisenhower

I mentioned it already in the previous chapter, but why is it so important to know how to prioritize?

Back in the day, when people lived by nature's cycles, they didn't need to plan their tasks or decide what was most important. Everything was categorized in advance by the simple fact that it had to coincide with nature's rhythm: sowing time, harvesting time, mating season, killing season, and so on. From sunup to sundown, there was very little margin for novelty or personal initiative, so there wasn't much use for agendas.

The freedom and disparity of today's lifestyles, on the other hand, do require that we prioritize if we want to do something worth doing. In the same way that a business that needs to hire a new worker can't select every candidate, you won't be able to do everything you would like to. You have to be selective. Some things will have to wait, and others will never happen.

I would love to sail around the world, but, all things considered, it's a wish I've discarded. I also want to learn another language, but for now it's not something I need to do, so it's not on my list of priorities.

I don't know anyone in the world with enough time to do all the things they wish they could. We have to choose, discard and prioritize.

Questions to ask yourself when prioritizing

Prioritizing is an exercise you need to do mindfully and with intention. The criteria for it are personal and different for everyone.

To figure out which tasks you need to put in first place, you first need to have a scale of preferences, an idea of which objectives are most important to you and what short- and long-term results each task will bring you.

If you're not clear on how to do this, I suggest that, when organizing your list of tasks for the week, you stop at each one and mentally respond:

1. What exactly does that task consist of?

Don't note down "meeting" in your agenda if it turns out that first you need to print off twenty reports, compare them with last year's and rehearse your pitch. If that's the case, that "meeting" is actually three separate tasks.

2. What are you doing that task for?

A task should only be done in order to obtain results. Even if it's being done for someone else, you need to do a results forecast. I don't mean you should be selfish or take advantage of people: of course, we do things for other people and out of love! What I mean is that you shouldn't do tasks just for the sake of it if they don't lead you anywhere.

Finally, sometimes you can only accept a valid result after you act, and sometimes it can be variable. If that's the case, what's the minimum acceptable for you?

3. How long will it take you to finish it?

If the task is new, you might not know exactly how long it will take you. But you should try to roughly work it out. If you think you will have to do it more times in the future, it's a good idea to note down how long you spent on it this time.

4. Does the task need to be done right away?

Is there something that requires your attention more urgently? If there are several obligations vying for your attention, compare them and make a decision. You might get this wrong, but it's always better than postponing them because you don't know what to tackle first.

5. How important is that task to your life goals?

Your everyday obligations shouldn't drown out your long-term aims. Of course, there will be entire days dedicated to completing urgent, obligatory tasks, but if your long-term goal is to prepare yourself to go into business on your own or become a writer, you need to make time for that.

The Eisenhower Method[5]

Also known as the Eisenhower Matrix, this method is a framework for ordering tasks depending on their urgency or importance in relation to your goals and other tasks they have to live alongside.

Its author devised it in the fifties, but it was recently talked about the Steven Covey's bestseller "The 7 Habits of Highly Effective People".

Basically, all your obligations, duties and responsibilities fall into two categories: urgent and important (or a combination of the two).

---

[5] Its name comes from the military officer Dwight D. Eisenhower, the 34th president of the United States.

Urgent tasks and important tasks:

- **Urgent tasks** are those which require your attention, but which don't necessarily add value or take you closer to your goals. In addition, their urgency is often subjective, so there is no real urgency. What's the difference?

Real urgency means that if the action is not carried out by a specific point, the consequences are too costly to be able to postpone that task.

On the other hand, **subjective urgency** is seen as urgent until something more urgent comes up, or something that is urgent for other people but not for you. No task of this type should come ahead of a real urgency.

- **Important tasks** are those that bring direct value to your goals. This value can be related to finance, security, family, commitment, growth, and so on. Often, they are long-term actions that are less concrete than urgent tasks ("take the car to the shop" is much clearer and more direct than "grow professionally"), so many important tasks end up being delayed because the urgent ones come first. You shouldn't make the mistake of giving them more time than they deserve.

The Eisenhower Matrix

The combination of the two gives rise to the Eisenhower Matrix. To use it, you need to be able to put all your tasks into one of the four quadrants:

1. Important and urgent tasks.

2. Important but not urgent tasks.

3. Urgent but not important tasks.

4. Tasks that are neither important nor urgent.

	Urgent	Not urgent
IMPORTANT		
NOT IMPORTANT		

Eisenhower Matrix

1. Important and urgent tasks:

These tasks must be done immediately due to their urgency and relevance. They are critical situations that may have a significant impact on your life or work if not tackled immediately. These tasks come under the DO category, and they are always the first on the list.

Example: attending to a family medical emergency.

2. Important but not urgent tasks:

These tasks are crucial for your long-term success, but they don't require immediate attention. The focus on this quadrant is proactive and contributes to your personal and professional development and the accomplishment of your objectives. These tasks come under the DECIDE category, because you still need to decide how and when the tasks will have to be done.

Example: Working out regularly to maintain a healthy lifestyle.

3. Urgent but not important tasks:

These should be done now and there will be negative consequences if they are not completed in a specific timeframe, but since they are not important (they don't add value to your objectives), you can find options for completing them, even if not yourself. These tasks fall under the DELEGATE field, because it's more useful and lucrative to pay someone to do them for you.

Example: Answering non-essential emails that require a quick response.

4. Tasks that are neither important nor urgent:

These tasks are only here to be detected and eliminated, leaving space for others. These tasks come under the ELIMINATE category.

Example: Scrolling social media with no specific purpose.

Factors to bear in mind when assessing your tasks:

Finally, some indirect factors can be the key to prioritizing a task or not:

- The economic impact, both positive (what you will earn or save) and negative (what it will cost you to tackle or leave that task).

- Time investment.

- The risk that task carries in terms of your chances of success or failure.

- Factors relating to health, social or environmental factors, and so on.

Chapter summary

Given that your day only has twenty-four hours, you should learn to prioritize.

– Often, we can be unclear on what tasks are a priority: urgent? Important? To decide, you can use methods like the Eisenhower Matrix.

– According to this method, there are four types of task, and this is the correct order for completing them:

1. Important and urgent tasks.

2. Important but not urgent tasks.

3. Urgent but not important tasks.

4. Tasks that are neither urgent nor important.

– Of these, the first type needs to be DONE now, the second needs to be SCHEDULED around a date, the third needs to be DELEGATED and the last ELIMINATED.

– Factors such as the economic impact (positive and negative), the consequences or risks for the rest of your objectives or wellbeing can be crucial when it comes to categorizing a task.

Avoid multitasking

"The shorter way to do many things is to only do one thing at a time."

— Mozart

We only have two hands and one brain. And they don't always work at 100%! So, while we can walk and chew gum at the same time, when tasks are more complicated than that, it can take its toll on the machinery. Why? Because multitasking isn't for humans, it's for robots.

We describe multitasking as the act of doing two or more tasks at the same time. We can also define it as the act of doing a single task while thinking about others.

Both practices are not advised by science as they are counterproductive. And although your instinct tells you that multitasking seems like a good way to save time, all studies show the opposite. Why? Because, in truth, **multitasking...doesn't exist**.

What do you mean, it doesn't exist? I do it every day!

In fact, you don't: when you do several tasks at once, your brain is moving its attention and executive functions from one task to the next at great speed. In other words: it doesn't divide or share out its resources between the tasks, but rather it goes quickly from one place to another. You force it to disconnect and reconnect to each task until the process is over. It's like having to cook several dishes at once, each in its own pot, but having to keep alternating them over a single burner.

Consequences of multitasking

Not only does multitasking exhaust your brain, it also makes it less lucid and less powerful:

- **You can't reach the same level of concentration.** You get to a much more superficial level that can open the door to mistakes.

- **It's harder to assimilate new information** because your brain is focused on not making mistakes when running from one task to another.

- **Your productivity levels go down** the longer the multitasking goes on: if your output when you first start multitasking is 10, as it goes on it will drop to 8, 7, 4, 3... 0.

- **Your level of commitment and involvement is much lower** and leads to demotivation and burnout faster.

- **There is less initiative and creativity,** since your brain is too busy to generate good ideas.

- **Multitasking multiplies your anxiety,** for the simple reason that it's tiring.

How to avoid multitasking

Now that you've decided to eliminate multitasking from your dynamics, here are some tips for avoiding it:

1. **Stick to your daily plan.** If necessary, count even the smallest task in order to avoid the temptation to overlap.

2. **Ignore things that "don't take much attention"** – phone notifications, TV, chatting with colleagues, laundry, and so on, until it's their turn.

3. **Be aware of when you want to start a new task** without finishing the previous one. Try to figure out why you suddenly want to change. Often, it's because the task you're doing doesn't seem to be going anywhere (you're driving too slowly due to traffic, so you check your phone), when it's boring, when you don't like it, when you're tired or when you're overwhelmed by the number of things you still have to do by the end of the day.

4. **Redirect your mind to the here and now** when you catch yourself thinking about things other than what you're doing right now.

5. **Ensure order in your house and workplace.** Ideally, you should have a space for each activity, so avoid working at the kitchen table, folding laundry in your office or arguing over the phone with your insurance company in bed: if you don't separate your

spaces, your chances of falling into multitasking go through the roof.

Multitasking is the enemy of excellence

If you look up from your daily multitasking and toward your life journey, in other words, the long term, you will realize that people who excel in any field have focused on that one and no other: Mozart stands out for his contribution to music, Marie Curie focused on radioactivity and Messi wasn't interested in anything other than being the best possible soccer player.

Would they have been as good if they had split their efforts between several professions that were equally demanding? I doubt it.

Many people believe themselves to be "experts" in several areas. I'm more of a "learner of everything, master in nothing". That's why, unless you have the intellectual skills and economic position of Leonardo da Vinci [6] , I recommend you focus on a single path.

The OHIO Method

Have you ever caught yourself checking your phone's weather app and then found that by one minute later you'd forgotten it? Or refreshing your email inbox five times an hour when once is more than enough?

Welcome to OHIO. OHIO stands for "Only Handle It Once": a focus I find very potent for avoiding repeating tasks, whether because you're thinking about other things or because you feel that the more times you do it, the safer it is.

Have you ever spent days, or weeks, moving the same objects in your house from one place to

---

[6] Hero of the Italian Renaissance, Leonardo da Vinci, was known as a sculptor, painter, inventor, anatomist, architect, designer, botanist, typographer, paleontologist, poet, engineer, optician, urbanist and philosopher, among other activities.

another over and over? I used to do it all the time. Next time, try OHIO. When you find objects not in their proper place, like clothes, kitchen utensils, paperwork and so on, instead of simply moving them, locate each object in its rightful place straight away. This way, you'll prevent disorder, keep your space tidy and save time and energy.

The idea behind the method is that when you tackle tasks immediately and complete them efficiently, you avoid an accumulation of work, reduce the time spent procrastinating and improve your general productivity.

Learn to delegate and to say no

Being efficient doesn't mean being able to do everything personally and on your own: being efficient also means knowing how to delegate and to say no when you need to.

If your boss asks you to work overtime this week to complete an important project, you should probably say yes in order to demonstrate responsibility and commitment. However, this gesture should not be taken as a permanent "yes" and it should be reciprocated.

If it happens again, suggest to your boss some compensation in the form of free time, for example (it can't and shouldn't always be a raise). This free time will enable you to attend to personal responsibilities or activities that you postponed due to the additional work. Make sure you balance your work and personal life so it's not constantly affecting your family, unless it's by prior agreement for a specific period of time.

When you set boundaries and communicate your needs, you ensure a healthier and more sustainable professional relationship in the long term.

In addition, it's crucial to learn to delegate, trust in others, work as a team and cooperate. These elements have been fundamental in our evolution as human beings. Delegating doesn't mean telling other people how to do tasks, but rather conceding that responsibility. Although you are still responsible for the final result, when you delegate you show trust in others, enabling them to act and make decisions. You should let go and allow things to be done.

Chapter summary

All research indicates that doing several tasks at once "to save time" is counterproductive and that we should avoid it. But how?

– Sequencing your list of tasks so that you don't begin one if you haven't finished the previous one.

– Redirecting your mind to the here and now every time you lose the thread because you're thinking about something else.

– Physically separating your different workspaces so you don't end up working in the kitchen, for example.

– Using the OHIO Method ("Only Handle It Once").

– Learning to delegate and to say no.

RULE N°6

Start with what's difficult

"Do the hard jobs first. The easy tasks will take care of themselves."

— Dale Carnegie

Like Dale Carnegie, Brian Tracy also advises us to "eat the biggest frog first"[7]. Why? Because if you start the day by swallowing a big fat frog, the rest of the day will seem easy. So, which task is that big frog?

The biggest frog is not the important task or one that brings value to your objectives and life: the fat frogs are the tasks that annoy you, those that put you in a bad mood and those that you're

---

[7] Brian Tracy is a Canadian writer and motivational speaker, author of paradigmatic works on personal development such as bestseller *Eat That Frog!* and *The Psychology of Selling*.

forced to do no matter what. They're the unpleasant tasks.

But...if those tasks put me in a bad mood, doesn't it make more sense to leave them until the end of the day?

Not at all. It's been proven that if you do them first, the fleeting bad mood passes and your motivation goes up for everything else, while if you leave those tasks till the end, your whole day will accumulate the negative energy they produce.

However, your impulse will be to start with what's easy, since more difficult tasks require more energy, concentration and commitment. This is where a definition of "difficult" comes into play.

What are the "difficult" tasks?

In general terms, your most difficult tasks are simply those you find the hardest to do. It has nothing to do with their level of objective complexity (an exercise in macroeconomics might be very difficult for a veterinarian but appealing to an economist), but what you find hard in terms of commitment, motivation, focus, uncertainty, interpretation of benefits, and so on. Sometimes, the most difficult task of a day could be a phone call.

What happens when you do the worst tasks first?

Remember we were saying that the tasks you postpone are still there, and their shadows keep getting longer? Well, when you decide to start with them, not only do you free yourself of that negative energy and the potential snowball effect of procrastination, you also get an extra dopamine hit.

Dopamine is one of the four hormones that give a sense of wellbeing (the other three being oxytocin, serotonin and endorphins) and it's linked to the brain's reward system.

Dopamine is what motivates us in the expectation of success, encourages us to strive to fulfil our goals and rewards us for a job well done with a "hit" of satisfaction. It's like a drug, but it's totally legal and healthy.

When we eat a frog, we get an extra dose of dopamine. When we don't (and this happens with any kind of procrastination), our dopamine levels go down and we become irritable and downhearted. In other words: not only do we not get the extra dose, we actually lose some of what we already had.

On the other hand, when we tackle the worst stuff first thing, we have a greater chance of success, since we're all clear and our batteries are charged. If we don't take advantage of that moment to take on the big frog, we risk spending the whole day anxious about doing that task, and if we don't end up tackling it, the same thing will happen all over again the next day. We will end up choking on the same frog day after day.

I know it's not always possible to start the day where you want to. If your frog is a very delicate meeting and it's at four o'clock in the afternoon, you can't just sleep in until three so you can do it first thing. What you need to do is begin the day by spending some time checking, rehearsing and visualizing that meeting, anticipating everything you're able to foresee.

This rehearsal will be enough to beat the frog, even if it's at four o'clock in the afternoon, when tiredness is starting to rear its head.

On the other hand, your personal successes have a memory and an accumulative power, meaning that when you get used to beginning with the difficult frog, those same frogs, however difficult, become less difficult as the months go on: you train yourself, and the dopamine is released almost effortlessly, even though you are making an effort.

How to motivate yourself to eat frogs for breakfast

Put it that way and it doesn't sound very appealing. However, it's not so bad. Let's take a look:

1. Remember that the frog's **shadow is bigger** than the frog itself.

2. Remember that once you "digest" the frog, it **releases dopamine** and that that dopamine gets easier and easier to get.

3. **Visualize the wellbeing** that awaits you for the rest of your day once you've dealt with your morning frogs.

4. Remember that you have **a greater chance of success** if you eat the frogs first thing in the morning: don't tempt fate!

5. Instead of feeling sorry for yourself, think about the people you admire and the **frogs they also had to eat to achieve their dreams**.

Chapter summary

This chapter can be summed up like this: begin with the biggest frog. And it's not just me saying that, but all experts in personal growth.

—   The biggest frogs aren't necessarily the more objectively complex, but those that we personally find hardest. These should be done first.

—   Fulfilling your least pleasant obligations first reduces your chances of failure, since it's in the first part of the day that you're most clear-headed and energetic.

—   When you eat the worst frogs first, your demotivation and bad mood disappear thanks to the dopamine, the wellbeing hormone linked to your reward system.

—   All of this makes the rest of your day's or week's tasks seem easier.

Make time to rest

"Laughter and reparative sleep keep the doctor away."

— Spanish saying

Some years ago, before becoming aware of the importance of good time management, I used to think that it was good to always keep busy. I thought that people who were constantly doing a thousand things were really making the most of life and should be emulated.

Over time, I realize that people who balanced their work time and their rest were wiser, happier and more efficient than those who never took a break.

However, when we talk to our friends and ask them what they've been doing, they tend to reply "lots of stuff", "really busy, you know", "up to here, like always". This can be interpreted as everything going well for them. But if you asked "what have you been doing?" and someone replied with "nothing", you'd be worried. You would think something was wrong: "Nothing? Are you sick? What happened?".

Being constantly busy has become a social status symbol, while enjoying free time is looked down upon. Why? Basically, because the idea of "going further" has been ingrained into us. It's as if we constantly had to demonstrate that our existence is "worth" something, that we're "in demand" and that we're indispensable, so don't get rid of us!

Of course, it's good to make the most of your time. Of course, you should aspire to go far. This book is about doing exactly that! But making the most of your time doesn't mean staying busy every minute. These are two different concepts.

As such, your logic shouldn't be: "This person works sixty hours a week, I'm sure they're very important". Your value as a human being shouldn't depend on how tired or stressed you are.

Rest according to science

Rest is no joke, nor is it something you can "adapt" to your needs. Recent discoveries in neurology show that a lack of rest (hours of sleep, leisure, relaxation, switch-off...) affects our brains in various ways: not only will you be more tired, in a worse mood and more prone to making mistakes, but it also reduces your prefrontal cortex. And that's big.

The prefrontal cortex is the part of your brain in charge of complex cognitive function (such as decision-making) and separates us from the simplest animals. The more evolved and intelligent an animal is, the bigger its prefrontal cortex. And when we subject it to continued stress and tiredness, that zone shrinks, which means your intelligence levels diminish.

Rest deprivation is considered a form of abuse, and sadly it has been used as a method of torture: when a prisoner is deprived of sleep, they soon begin to suffer from hallucinations and other problems. Three days straight without sleep bring you closer to dementia and death from heart failure.

On the other hand, protecting your rest time (not just sleep, but also time for relaxation, leisure, contemplation or just doing nothing) not only makes you more productive, it also makes you a better person.

When you rest, you don't lose time – you gain it.

Start by disciplining your nights

Sleep is a basic need, but millions of people don't or can't sleep well, and not enough of them take the problem seriously.

Why don't we rest as much as we should?

Most people report the same reasons: stress, anxiety, physical pain, worries, imbalance between mental and physical tiredness, excessive stimulation, light, noise, and so on. However, I doubt that we have worse sleep conditions than in the Middle Ages, for example.

That's what I tell my patients – not to belittle their concerns but to **put them into perspective**. I don't tell them that their anxiety or pain is not important, just that they are not important when climbing into bed at night. Simply put, they're not useful.

Any thought or emotion that comes into your head when you've already decided to sleep is working against you and you need to be able to push it away.

The notepad on your nightstand

Some patients tell me that it's in bed that they remember the most important things they need to do the following day or that they suddenly get a brainwave. Others tell me that worries creep in right when they're going to bed. This happens because your nervous system is so **destabilized** by stress that it resists sleep "in case there's something else to do". It's permanently **on the alert.**

A good way of telling your brain it can relax now is to keep a pad on your nightstand and write down any thoughts that come into your head. A couple of words is enough. What you're telling your hypervigilance is "Okay, noted, you can sleep, we'll deal with that tomorrow".

As soon as you start to use this technique, your brain gets used to turning off the ideas running round your head right when you're going to sleep, because it knows you've noted it down for the next day and that you won't forget about it.

The difficult job of melatonin

Melatonin is a hormone we release naturally and which affects our sleep cycles. Its levels increase at nightfall, when the light dies, and begin to descend after the first few hours of sleep. Melatonin peaks **between 8pm and 10pm** (it varies a little depending on the season and your geographical location). So, that's when you need to be ready to go to sleep.

The function of melatonin is to facilitate the **latency phase**, which is the time you need to go from being awake to asleep (the dreaded "falling asleep" stage). A sleep latency of up to twenty minutes is considered normal for children and young people and up to thirty minutes for adults and elderly people.

To help it fulfil its role, you need to make things easy for it:

- Respect your bedtime routine.

- End the day with a guided relaxation exercise for sleep.

- Keep to the same schedule every day.

- Turn the bedroom into a nice, calm, tidy place with the right temperature and no devices at night.

- Give the latency phase time: if you want to sleep for seven and a half hours, don't go to bed right when you have seven and a half hours left before your alarm. All you will do is get nervous as the minutes tick by and you're still awake.

Leisure is obligatory

Relaxation activities are supposed to liberate and refresh your mind. But in this production system we've created, even pleasure activities have become a race against the clock to rack up "experiences" and "memories" in order to keep up with no one in particular.

I hope it's okay if I tell you the story of a married couple with two children who lived next door to me. One summer, when they got back from vacation, the guy told me they had had the best vacation since they'd been married.

It turned out that every year, one of the two of them would plan the vacation, and that year it was his wife's turn. They had a good budget, the fruit of months of hard work, but they were both physically and mentally exhausted. So when the wife revealed what she had organized, the husband was quaking in his boots: first of all, they were going to take a fourteen-hour flight with two stopovers to their destination, then they were going to do a walking tour with other people and change accommodation every three days in order to explore every corner of the country. It was perfect, his wife had explained, because even though they had to get up every day at six o'clock and climb on a bus with the kids, they were going to make the most of every minute.

The husband was so overwhelmed that it took him a minute to realize that she was yanking his chain. What she had actually planned was a vacation where they could *really* rest. They were going to a hotel not far from where they lived, with enough attractions that they wouldn't be bored but with no obligations. The kids would be in their element, and so would they. They could come back whenever they want, stay with people they wanted to see (or not), and do whatever they pleased.

So that's what they did.

When they got home, glowing and rejuvenated, all their friends were surprised: "Is that all you did?" they asked, disappointed. They were expecting some great trip. But it had been!

The concept of leisure varies from one person to another, one life stage to another and one set of circumstances to another. But it should never be interpreted as a way of satisfying other people's expectations or following trends. On the contrary: it's a time for enriching your soul, making peace with the world and reestablishing your balance. The competition to see who collects the most "extraordinary experiences" around the world to post to Instagram – leave that to others.

How to create leisure and rest time

We often believe that leisure time doesn't need to be planned, because it just happens. It's all the time we have "free".

But it doesn't work that way. If you don't plan out your leisure, rest, relaxation and rebalance time, it simply won't exist, although your need for rest will still be there. The outcome is burnout, sooner or later.

Below, I'm going to give you some guidelines for dealing with your rest time as just as valuable as your productive time:

1. Do some leisure brainstorming.

One of the biggest problems in creating leisure time is that people don't really know what they want to do with their free time. They end up doing what other people do, or whatever involves the least thought. Any activity, no matter how simple it is, is valid if it gives you time to switch off, but not if while you're doing it, you're thinking about what a waste of time it is rather than enjoying it.

That's why I suggest you do a brainstorm of activities that appeal to you, without worrying about economic limitations, real possibilities and so on. The objective is to discover what you actually want to do. A pizza and movie night (this is my favorite), a diving trip, going to see the planes at the airport with your daughter, getting a massage, an afternoon of creative cooking, watching an active volcano, taking guitar lessons, a concert two hundred miles away…anything that would free your mind from stress counts.

Also be careful that you're not noting down activities just to brag about a fearless life or prove something to someone.

2. Shortlist.

Then, assess your list according to what's possible, what you feel like doing and what your current situation is.

Choose some activities to do:

- Every day (listening to music, reading an article that's caught your eye, making a little purchase...)

- Every week (a yoga session, a music class, a hike...)

- Every month.

- Every year.

- Once in your lifetime.

This list, in addition to being the first step to safeguarding your relaxation activities, helps you to look forward to them, which prolongs your enjoyment of them.

3. Schedule dates for your chosen activities.

Remember that leisure activities should be very appealing to you: if, when the time comes, you would rather just lay on the couch, figure out where you've gone wrong.

If necessary, sacrifice some obligations: I'm sure there are dispensable tasks or tasks that could be made lighter or even postponed. I don't mean shirk your responsibilities, just find some balance between work time and rest time.

4. Automatize the actions that lead you to your leisure time.

To avoid the activities that most excite you getting left on your agenda and never truly happening, you need to pave the way for them.

For example: planning a relaxing day at the beach should be simple. If it takes you forty-five prior tasks (renting a car, swapping your shift at work, preparing food, buying toiletries, figuring out where the beach towels are, delaying tasks you would prefer to finish soon, and so on), that activity will become a source of stress rather than a fun one.

Wherever possible, make the path easier in advance.

5. Create long-term leisure goals.

William Lyon Phelps once said: "Those who decide to use leisure as a means of mental development, who love good music, good books, good pictures, good plays, good company, good conversation – what are they? They are the happiest people in the world."

What I mean by long-term leisure goals is activities that involve progress: ones you can go into depth on. For example, if you're curious and ancient architecture, you would likely enjoy it more and more as you get to know it. If you love cooking, the long-term objective is to enjoy preparing increasingly personal and creative.

I can tell you that this type of leisure, when it's done for yourself and not only for the satisfaction of learning, is the best kind. So don't forget to pick an objective of this kind for your life. It can be learning to speak a language or play an instrument, cooking, writing poetry or flying light aircraft: anything that you can make progress in.

Chapter summary

–   Rest is essential not only for recharging your batteries, but also for connecting to the meaning of life itself.

–   That said, we are all expected to rest as little as possible, just enough not to get sick or collapse. Don't fall into that trap!

–   You can learn to rest and enjoy life. First, you need to stop believing that time for enjoyment will magically appear on your schedule. You have to plan it like any other task.

–   You must prioritize good sleep habits, whatever it takes.

–   Leisure is not a trend or a privilege: it's a necessary kind of time that connects you to yourself. That's why it's so important to respect it and not to subject yourself to external expectations.

–   Long-term leisure contributes to your happiness.

Toward a happier, more productive future

Well, this is where we say goodbye for now.

You've walked an incredible journey on which you've acquired powerful tools and strategies for taking control of your time and your life. The "simple" fact that you have come this far proves that. Did you know that a large percentage of people don't finish the books they start? So...CONGRATULATIONS! You're on the right track!

Now, you need to keep applying the 7 rules for time management to your everyday life. You'll see how, little by little, they start to come naturally to you and become a part of who you are.

Don't ever give up; keep moving forward with enthusiasm and determination. With your new focus and improved skills, you can achieve everything you set your mind to. Remember that every day is a new opportunity to achieve your dreams.

You alone are the captain of your time and you have the power to decide how to want to live; enjoy every moment of life. If you follow your path with passion and determination, great accomplishments await you alongside a life full of joy and satisfaction.

You can achieve everything you want to. Your future is in your hands!

Hugs
Daniel

Your opinion is very important

As I'm an independent author, your opinion is so important to me and to future readers like you. I would be hugely grateful if you would leave me **a review on your favorite store** to tell me what you thought of my book **so that I can keep on improving it**:

- What did you like best?
- Is there anything you felt was missing
- Who would you recommend it to?
- ...

www.danieljmartin.es/review/pot

A gift just for you!

Would you like to **read my next book completely FREE**? Scan the code below and **join my readers' club!**

Great surprises await: be the first to read my new releases, listen to my audiobooks for free, get signed and dedicated copies... and much more!

www.danieljmartin.es/readersclub/

Other books by Daniel J. Martin

www.danieljmartin.es/wide/books